Say it in

SCOTTISH

Say it in Scots

SCOTTISH
PLACE-NAMES

Maggie Scott

BLACK & WHITE PUBLISHING

First published 2008
by Black & White Publishing Ltd
99 Giles Street, Edinburgh EH6 6BZ

ISBN: 978 1 84502 193 1

1 3 5 7 9 10 8 6 4 2   08 09 10 11 12

A CIP catalogue record for this book is available from the British Library.

Typeset by Ellipsis Books Ltd
Printed and bound by Nørhaven Paperbacks A/S

Contents

Say it in Scots

Whether you are a Scots speaker already, or whether you are a visitor to Scotland, this series of books is guaranteed to awaken your enthusiasm for the Scots language. There is bound to be something in these books to interest you. They are based on the *Scottish National Dictionary* and *A Dictionary of the Older Scottish Tongue*, which are now available online at **www.dsl.ac.uk** as the *Dictionary of the Scots Language*. Additional material comes from the ongoing research of Scottish Language Dictionaries, who are responsible for the stewardship of these great reference works and for keeping the record of Scots words up to date.

Scots is the language of Lowland Scotland and the Northern Isles. It is also used in parts of Ulster. Along with English and Gaelic, it is one of Scotland's three indigenous languages. Scots is descended from Northern

Old English, itself greatly influenced by Old Scandinavian. From the twelfth century onwards, it became increasingly established in Lowland Scotland and was then enriched by words borrowed from French, Latin, Gaelic and Dutch. It was the language of government, spoken by kings, courtiers, poets and the people. It has a literary heritage the equal of any in Europe.

Like any other language, it has its own dialects such as Glaswegian, Ayrshire, Shetland, Doric, Border Scots, etc. These have a rich diversity and share a central core uniting them as varieties of the Scots language. We have tried to reflect the history and variety of Scots in these books and hope you will find some words that you can savour on your tongue and slip into everyday conversation.

Some of the spelling, especially in the older quotations, may be unfamiliar, but if you try reading the quotations out loud, you will find they are not difficult to understand.

Chris Robinson

Director

Scottish Language Dictionaries

www.scotsdictionaries.org.uk

Introduction

This book takes a look at a variety of Scots terms that have been used to describe Scotland's hills, valleys, rivers, settlements and streets. Each entry discusses a Scots word that can be found in the *Dictionary of the Scots Language* and explores its connections with the landscape. Because this book focuses on the Scots language, you will not find all of Scotland's place-names in it. Instead, you will find many Scots terms that are central to Scotland's culture.

Many Scottish place-names have been coined in Gaelic, rather than Scots, or in languages that are now no longer spoken, including Old Norse and Old English. Others were coined in the Celtic language from which modern Welsh is descended, which was spoken in Scotland until the tenth century. Various different terms have been used for this language, including 'British' and 'Brittonic' and 'Brythonic', and the Celtic scholar Kenneth Jackson introduced the concept of separating the 'Cumbric' of southern Scotland from the 'Pictish' of north-eastern Scotland. It may be more accurate (and more straightforward) to describe it as 'early Welsh', but in this book I have adopted the convention of using 'P-Celtic', distinguishing it from the 'Q-Celtic' family of languages that includes Irish Gaelic, Scottish Gaelic and Manx. Another group of names that deserves special mention is river-names. Some of these are so old that they may have been coined before the Celtic languages split away from their Indo-European parent language, which is the common ancestor of most of Europe's modern languages.

Besides the ancient river-names, many of Scotland's best-known places are not Scots in origin. **Glasgow** is of P-Celtic origin and is made up of *glas* 'green', a term shared with Gaelic, and *cau* 'hollow', from which modern Welsh *cau* is descended. **Perth** is also from P-Celtic, and if you know the Welsh word *perth* 'bush, thicket, copse', you will quickly see the connection.

[4]

Gaelic was spoken all over Scotland at one time, and has left its mark in many place-names, particularly in the north and west. **Inverness** is from Gaelic *inbhir nis*, and marks the site of the mouth of the river Ness, *inbhir* signifying a confluence.

Many of the Scots terms discussed in this book are derived from other languages including Gaelic and Old Norse, and in some instances both the Scots term and its Celtic or Scandinavian 'parent' have been used to coin Scottish place-names. In the case of hill-names that incorporate the term *knock*, for example, it may be that the name is a Scots coinage, or it may be that the name is an original Gaelic formation, in which the Gaelic term *cnoc*, from which the Scots is derived, was used to coin the name. Further research is needed in order to analyse the name's development.

When investigating the history of a name in order to draw some conclusion about its origin, it is necessary to look at all of the known historical spellings of the name, since names can alter radically during their lifetimes. The majority of Scottish place-names have been in existence since the Middle Ages and some (especially river-names) are considerably older. In his seminal work, *Scottish Place-Names* (2001), Professor W. F. H. Nicolaisen examines the history of the name Falkirk, tracing its evolution back to the twelfth century and charting its variant spellings in Gaelic, Latin and Scots. In Scots, Falkirk was often spelled *Faukirk* (1298, 1391, 1468, etc.) or *Fawkirk* (1391, 1392, 1537, etc.) and spellings with -*l*- are not recorded until the fifteenth century. The name may be translated as 'variegated church', from Middle Scots *faw* 'of various colours' and Scots *kirk* 'church'. As Professor Nicolaisen points out, the later re-spellings with *Fal-* appear to represent an attempt to 'correct' the spelling, in recognition that Scots tends to drop the letter *l* in favour of this pronunciation (compare *ba', baw* 'ball'; *ca', caw* 'call'). This same phenomenon is seen in the historical spellings of the word *chaumer* 'room, chamber'. In the sixteenth century, the word was frequently re-spelled as *chalmer*, as though the spelling *chaumer* (perfectly good Scots) reflected some sort of error.

The example of the history of Falkirk should serve to demonstrate that the study of place-names can involve many different languages and a great deal of painstaking research. What you will find in this book is a distillation of some of that research as it applies to the Scots terms that have been used to name our rural and urban landscapes.

It has become traditional in place-name studies to refer to the county names that pertained before the reorganisation of local government in the 1970s, and this convention has been observed here. A useful summary of the changes in governmental organisation is provided by the Department of Geography at the University of Edinburgh:

http://www.geo.ed.ac.uk/home/scotland/localgovt.html

Further Reading

Gelling, M., W. F. H. Nicolaisen & M. Richards, eds (1970), *The Names of Towns and Cities in Britain*, London: Batsford.

Nicolaisen, W. F. H. (2001), *Scottish Place-Names*, Edinburgh: John Donald.

Scott, M. (2003), 'Scottish Place-Names', in John Corbett et al. eds, *The Edinburgh Companion to Scots*, Edinburgh: Edinburgh University Press.

Taylor, S., ed. (1998), *The Uses of Place-Names*, Edinburgh: Scottish Cultural Press.

1 Hills and Mountains

Many of Scotland's highest lands are located in the north and west of the country, in areas traditionally associated with Gaelic culture. It will therefore come as no surprise that a great number of the Scots terms for geographical features associated with hills and mountains are derived from Gaelic, though other languages are also involved. The debt that Scots owes to Gaelic is considerable, as this chapter will demonstrate.

Balloch – this term for a narrow mountain pass is derived from Gaelic *bealach*, with the same meaning.

The spelling of the word is sometimes closer to its Gaelic original, which is often represented in place-names. James Hogg uses it in his poem *Farewell to Glen-Shalloch* (1828):

I'll sing thee to rest In the balloch untrodden.

Bard – in Shetland, a bard is a bold headland, the top of which projects beyond its base. Several examples of the term can be found in Shetland place-names, including the Bard o Bressay and the Bard o Mousa. The word is derived from Old Norse *barð*, which denoted both the edge of a hill and the prow of a ship, and probably entered the Shetland dialect via Norn, the Scandinavian-derived language that was spoken in the islands up until the late eighteenth century.

Ben – Scotland's bens and glens are well known for their beauty. Scots *ben* is derived from Gaelic *beann*, found in the names of such major Scottish mountains as Ben Cruachan, Ben Lomond and Ben Nevis. Binns in West Lothian is also derived from a form of the same

Gaelic word. This ben is of course different from the *ben* of a **but-and-ben**, the traditional Scottish two-roomed house, where the *ben* was the inner or 'best' room.

Brae – the *Banks and Braes o' Bonnie Doon* and the *Braes o' Ballochmyle* have been immortalised in song by Robert Burns. A brae can be a hillside, or a bank of a river or lake, though in street-names it usually denotes a road with a steep gradient. There are Braeheads and Braefoots (but not Braefeet) throughout the country. The origin of the word is not straightforward. Old English *brū eyebrow,* 'brow; brow of a hill' and its Old Norse sister-form *brá* are involved, but Gaelic *bràighe* 'the upper part of something' has also played a role, particularly in names like the Braes of Angus. In figurative use, something that has gone *doun the brae* has fallen to wrack and ruin.

Cairn – Scots *cairn*, from Gaelic *càrn*, has denoted a pile of stones since the Middle Ages, as demonstrated by this quotation from the *Rental Book of the Cistercian Abbey of Cupar-Angus* (1557):

The croft of land callit the well medow . . . is
devidit be carnis of stanis.

In Scots it can also indicate a stony hill. Such areas are not always conducive to cultivation, as in this Banffshire quotation from the *Dictionary of the Scots Language*:

His placie lay at the fit o' the cairn o' the Ord, an'
wiz maistly gey peer grun.

Craig – denoting a crag, cliff, or projecting spur of rock, *craig* is found in the names of many coastal places including Ailsa Craig in the Firth of Clyde, famous for the curling stones made from its granite. Scots *craig* is derived from Gaelic *creag*, so names with the modern spelling *craig* may reflect either an original Scots or an original Gaelic name.

Dod – although this is an everyday Scots word for a lump of something, it takes on a more specific meaning in place-names, where it usually refers to a bare hill with a rounded top. Scottish examples include Deuchrie Dod and Wester Dod in the Lammermuir Hills though there are several plain old Dod Hills in the Borders.

Dun – some of the best known locations with place-names incorporating Gaelic *dùn* 'fort, castle' (or its P-Celtic sister-form *din)* have been inhabited for thousands of years. Before Old English-speaking invaders captured Edinburgh in the seventh century, the settlement that was to become Scotland's capital city was known as *Dùn-Èideann*, but the name was altered in the wake of this conquest to include Old English *burh* 'fortified enclosure'.

The term *dun* was borrowed by non-Gaelic speakers in the sense 'pre-historic fort', and is found in the *Statistical Account of Scotland* for Argyll (1791–9):

> *Duns are very numerous, not only in this, but in all parishes in the Highlands.*

Fell – there are many hill and mountain names that incorporate the term *fell*, such as Goat Fell on Arran and the Campsie Fells north of Glasgow. *Fell* derives from Old Norse and has been recorded in Scots since the fifteenth century.

Heugh – although resembling a ceilidh dancer's enthusiastic exclamation, this word typically denotes a precipice, a cliff, a steep bank, or a glen or ravine with overhanging sides. It is sometimes spelled *heuch* and is derived from Old English *hōh* meaning 'heel'. In Scots place-names, it often combines with names for birds, as in Corbie Heugh in the Borders (from Scots *corbie* 'crow, raven'), Earn's Heugh near Aberdeen (from Scots earn 'eagle') and Ravensheugh in Lothian.

Hill – in Scotland, the word *hill* may be used of all kinds of landscape features from high mountains to artificial mounds. There are many examples of the name Hillfit or Hillfoot in Scotland, denoting either the ground at the foot of a hill, or foot-hills. The best-known example is perhaps the Hillfoots that form the district at the base of the Ochil Hills in Clackmannanshire, running eastwards from Stirling, beyond Dollar.

Kip – a kip is usually a pointed hill, and the word *kip* has a variety of other meanings relating to pointed things that point upwards — cattle described as *kippie* have upturned horns, and someone who is *kip-nebbit* has an upturned nose. Several hills have the straightforward designation 'The Kip' and in the Pentland Hills are East and West Kip. The term is thought to be related to Middle Dutch *kippe* and Middle Low German *kippe* meaning *point*, 'peak, tip'.

Knap – usually denoting a hillock or knoll in Scots, this term comes into use in place-names by a variety of different routes as it has parallels in many different languages. Hills called *knap* may be derived from either Old English *cnæpp* 'top, summit' or Gaelic *cnap* 'knob', which may itself be a borrowing from Old Norse *knappr* 'knob, rounded top'. A well-known literary example is

Peesie's Knap in Lewis Grassic Gibbon's *Sunset Song* (1932), where the first part of the name is the Scots word *peesie* 'lapwing'.

Knock – this Scots term for a hill is derived from Gaelic *cnoc* 'hillock', found in names such as Knockhill in Fife. Here, the original name — *Knock* — has been modified by the later addition of *-hill*. Such changes provide insights into Scotland's history, and in this case it seems that a wave of immigrants who knew little or no Gaelic decided to reform the name to mean *the hill at Knock*, unaware that Knock also meant 'hill'.

Knowe – a knowe is usually a small knoll or hilltop, but some are considerably more substantial. Fifescar Knowe in the Manor Hills rises to a height of over 800 metres. This word is used in Scots and northern English, and like its southern cousin *knoll*, derives from Old English *cnoll*. Knowes can be found in Scottish literature, as in Robert Burns' poem *Ca' the yowes to the knowes* (1794) and Sir Walter Scott's description in his novel, *The Black Dwarf* (1816), of the *'bonny broomy knowe'.*

Law – derived from Old English *hlǣw* 'mound, cairn, hill, mountain', this term is frequently found in the place-names of southern and eastern Scotland, in areas most directly affected by medieval settlers from northern England. Some well-known Scottish laws are Dundee Law, Largo Law, Berwick Law and Broad Law. Also weel-kent is Traprain Law in Lothian, where early twentieth-century archaeologists discovered a significant hoard of Roman silver artefacts, now in the care of the Royal Museum of Scotland.

Mounth – the word is derived from Gaelic *monadh* 'mountain range', and can also denote hilly barren country or high ground. When used in the phrase *The Mounth,* it describes the mountains of the eastern Highlands, specifically the eastern Grampians of Angus and Kincardineshire, south of the Dee. Spellings of the name have varied over time, and *month* is common in older texts. The medieval *Asloan Manuscript* reports that *Malcome Canmor . . . chasit* (chased) *Makbeth our* (over) *the Month to Lumfannane.*

Nabb – also sometimes spelled *knabb*, this word for a hillock or summit is often found in place-names in Shetland and Orkney and is of Scandinavian origin. Related etymologically to Scots *neb* 'nose', it also refers to features that stick out, including a rocky headland near Lerwick known simply as The Knab.

Noup – derived from a Scandinavian word of similar meaning, a *noup* is a jutting or overhanging crag or mountain-top, or a steep headland or promontory. The word is known mainly in Orkney and Shetland, and is found in a number of Shetland place-names including the Noop of Noss, which features in *Echoes from Klingrahool* (1898), by the poet 'Junda' (James Stout Angus):

> *The moon hangs over the Noop of Noss*
> *Like a golden shield with a silver boss.*

Pap – this term frequently denotes a conical hill. The most famous examples are probably the Paps of Jura and the Pap of Glencoe, though the latter has developed fairly recently as a modern nickname for the kenspeckle mountain dominating the familiar tourist views of Glen Coe. It is also known by its Gaelic name Sgorr na Cìche.

Pen – although no longer in use as a general Scots word, *pen* was used until at least the nineteenth century to indicate a pointed, conical hill. The term derives from a P-Celtic word, and is the ancestor of modern Welsh *pen* 'head'. Place-names with *pen* include Ettrick Pen, Skelfhill Pen and Pennygant Hill near Hawick in the Borders.

Pike – although not especially frequent in Scottish place-names, there are a number of pikes in the Borders, including The Pike in Roxburgh and Pike Fell near Langholm. There are many pikes in the English Lake District and, *pike* being of Scandinavian origin, it is no surprise that the distribution of these place-names corresponds to the areas of Britain that saw heavy Anglo-Scandinavian settlement in the Middle Ages.

Pobie – this term for a peak or high hill is only found in Shetland place-names and is Scandinavian in origin. A 1903 quotation recorded in the *Dictionary of the Scots Language* from Joseph Wright's *English Dialect Dictionary* provides the following information:

> Fishermen all round these islands speak of the 'Pobies o' Unst', i.e. Saxavord Hill, 'da Muckle Pobie,' and the Hjoag o' Crusifell, 'Pobie littla'.

Such names are not always recorded on maps, although they are often well known locally.

Riggin – although this word has several other meanings, including *the ridge of a roof* and *the backbone of a person or animal*, it can also denote a high ridge of land, especially a crest of high land running along the side of a plain. It is also found in the compound *sky-riggin*, a ridge of land seen against the skyline. Examples of this term in place-names include the Riggin o' Fife, which divides the northern part of the county from the south.

Scaur – a scaur or scar is usually a sheer rock or precipice, or a steep eroded hill. Kippford near Kirkcudbright is known locally as The Scaur, and the Scaur o' Doon Road in Ayr is named after the steep bank of the River Doon. The term is sometimes applied to a bank of gravel stretching out from the shore, as in Howgarth Scar and Powfoot Scar in Dumfries and Galloway.

Scurran – this term of Gaelic origin is used of a peak or pinnacle on a hill, specifically of Ben Rinnes in Banffshire. James Brown's Morayshire text *The Round Table Club* (1873) includes the following account:

I hae thocht many a time aboot that mysel' fin' I wis

herdin' sheep, an' lookin' at the scurrans o' the hill-heid. The top of the mountain has been worn down by the weather leaving this scurran as a remnant.

Seat – there are a number of prominent Scottish landmarks that incorporate this term, including the imposing Arthur's Seat in Edinburgh, and Earl's Seat in the Campsie Fells. Seat is one of the many everyday words (alongside *egg*, *husband*, *skirt*, *outlaw*, etc.) that was borrowed into English and Scots from Old Norse.

Shank – words for parts of the body are often used figuratively to indicate the shapes of specific features in the landscape. *Shank*, as a term meaning 'leg', is used in place-names to describe the downward spur or slope of a hill. In some cases, as in the Shank of Inchgrundle in the Grampians, the term has been added to an older Gaelic name, but names like Shankend Hill in the Borders reflect use of terminology shared between Scots and English.

Shin – like **shank**, shin is found in the names of places that resemble that part of the body, usually ridges of steep hillsides, or projecting areas of high ground. From its name, Catcleugh Shin in the Scottish Borders may once have been the haunt of wildcats. George Watson's *Roxburghshire Word Book* (1923) also notes the use of *shin-end* as a term for the lower end of the slope of a hill.

Shouder – Scots for *shoulder*, the word *shouder* is used of a rounded part of a hill. In *Mang Howes and Knowes* (1925), Eliot Cowan Smith describes his view of Ruberslaw:

keekin bye the shooder o the Dunion.

Gaelic *gualainn* 'shoulder' is found in the mountain names Màm na Gualainn and Gualainn nan Osna.

Sneug – this is a Shetland term for a protrusion in the landscape and may denote a hump-like projection, slope or a round summit. On the Island of Foula, the westernmost of the Shetland Islands, there are five major peaks, the tallest of which is called The Sneug.

Tap – also found in its anglicised form *top*, this term for a summit is found in place-names including the Tops of Craigeazle in Dumfries and Galloway. In Aberdeenshire, another hill-top is known as the Tap o' Noth, and one of the peaks of Bennachie is known as the Mither Tap.

Torr – in place-names, this term usually represents Gaelic *tòrr* 'hill'. Although the word *torr* was borrowed by Scottish writers, it has only rarely been recorded in historical literature and is not known to have been used to coin names in Scots. It is often found in Gaelic place-names, such as Tarbrax in Lanarkshire. The second part of this place-name is from Gaelic *breac* 'speckled'. In the case of Tarbolton in Ayrshire, however, the Gaelic term has been added to the earlier name *Bolton*, derived from Old English.

As you will by now have gathered, the topography of Scotland is made up of a tapestry of different languages, and although parts of the picture are still visible (as in transparent names such as Hillfoot or Knock), there are many areas where time and cultural interaction have blurred the images. Investigating the early spellings of a name to determine its origin and meaning can be very interesting, but does not always produce conclusive results.

2 Rivers and Lochs

Many of Scotland's major rivers have very ancient names, some of which are Celtic, but some of which date back before the time of the Celts. These oldest names are thought to belong to an early stage of the development of the Indo-European family of languages, before the Celtic and Germanic branches went their separate ways. The early Celtic or Indo-European names include the Spey, the Tay, the Tweed, the Ness, the Dee, the Avon, the Ayr and the lost river-name *Adder* (found in the modern names Blackadder and Whiteadder in the Borders).

Aber – instantly recognisable as the first component of such names as Aberdeen and Aberfeldy, *aber*, 'confluence, river-mouth' is the P-Celtic equivalent of the Gaelic word *inbhear*, which appears in Scottish place-names in the form **inver**. Because of its northern distribution, *aber* is sometimes classified as 'Pictish', along with other P-Celtic terms such as *pert* 'wood, copse', the ancestor of modern Welsh *perth* 'bush, copse'.

Burn – this is one of the most frequently used Scots words for a small river, and is found in the names of more than 2,500 streams across the country. Although *burn* is usually preceded by a descriptive term, as in names like Whiteburn or Blackburn, there is also a large group of names that use the construction *Burn of* followed by another term, usually a place-name in its own right. Examples include Burn of Achlais in Stirlingshire, Burn of Birse in Aberdeenshire and Burn of Crockadale in Shetland.

Doachs – this term is applied specifically to the rocky stretch of the River Dee at Tongland in Kirkcudbrightshire. In 1926, Joseph Robison described the local topography:

> *The hill slopes steeply to the south and east, where the Dee . . . enters the rocky gorge of the Doachs.*

The name Doachs is derived from Gaelic *dabhach* in the sense 'vat, tub', although another meaning of the word is 'a measure or land', which in Scots has become *davach* or *davoch* and is generally restricted to the north and east.

Dub – in place-names, *dub* often refers to a pond or pool, particularly one that is muddy or contains stagnant water. Examples include the Glasgow street-name Goosedubs and the farm-name Blackdubbs in Armadale, West Lothian. More generally, a *dub* can also be a puddle, and someone described as a *dub-skelper* travels rapidly regardless of the state of the roads.

Ess – this term for a waterfall is more frequently found in place-names than in other written contexts, though it does appear in a small number of quotations documented by the *Dictionary of the Scots Language*. These include, from David Macdonald's *The Mountain Heath* (1838): *the hoarse murmur of the stream, That fed the rapid ess.*

The word derives from Gaelic *eas* 'waterfall', and is found in the Bridge of Ess in Aberdeenshire and the Ess of Glen Latterach in Morayshire. The Irish Gaelic form is also found in such names as the Ess-na-Larach, or 'Mare's Waterfall' in Glenarrif, County Antrim.

Flush – although it may not be unusual to associate the word 'flush' with the word 'bog', this particular *flush* is used of boggy or swampy ground, or a pool of water in a field. The derivative *floshen* is used to describe a large, shallow puddle, as in the following passage from the *Scots Magazine* (1823):

I could see peat-mosses on all hands, filled with peat-stacks, and, occasionally, pretty large floshens, or collections of moss-water.

Fluther – found in place-names such as Fluthers Wood in Fife, and also in some northern English names, this term denotes a marsh or boggy piece of ground. It may be related to Scots *flude* and English *flood*, and is known to have been used in Scots texts since the early seventeenth century. *The Book of the Thanes of Cawdor* (1611) describes

The fludder or myre upon the south side of the common muir (moor).

Garth – this term for a shallow part of a river, or a stretch of shingle used as a ford, occurs in the compound *garth-fishing* which describes the fishing of such places. As a place-name term, *garth* is found in such names as Garthdee and Inchgarth in Aberdeenshire. That said, in place-names, *garth* can also be an enclosure, yard, or area of cultivated land, so when you see a name containing *garth* it may have a different connotation.

Grain – generally used as a term for a branch or fork of a river, this word can also be applied to an arm of the sea. In Robert Chambers' *Popular Rhymes of Scotland* (1826), the specific topography of a place called *Deadman's Grain* is described as the *junction of two small mountain rills which happen to meet in a forked manner*. This word is derived from Old Norse *grein* meaning *branch (of a tree, of the sea), division*.

Gullion – a gullion is a term for a quagmire, marsh or swamp, as described in the following quotation from John MacTaggart's *Scottish Gallovidian Encyclopedia* (1824):

He'd slonk adown, or ere he ken'd,
A miry, quacking quaw,
Or glauroch, far aboon the knee,
Through some blue rashy gullion.

A gullion can also be a pool of soft mud, manure, decayed vegetable matter or any mushy substance, especially one found on farmland. In Matthew Mulcaghey's *Ballymulcaghey* (1929) there is a typical illustration:

Down he went on the whole broad of his back in yon gullion at the byre dure.

Inver – clearly recognisable as the first component of such names as Inveraray, Inverness and Inverkip, this term denotes either a confluence where two streams meet, or the mouth of a river, and is the Gaelic equivalent of P-Celtic **aber**. Although most often found in place-names, *inver* has made rare appearances in Scots sources as an independent word with the same sense. For example, in an entry for 1766 in the *Records of Invercauld*, there is a description of a confluence:

a small stripe or burn runs down the same, to the Inver of the said small stripe or burn into the burn of little Cairntagert.

Lane – when applied to rivers, this term denotes a slow-moving, meandering stream. Evidence for the word is found mainly in the south-west of Scotland and it is used to form several place-names in Galloway including Lanebreddan and Lanemannoch. It is thought to derive from Gaelic *lèan* 'marshy meadow'. A somewhat unflattering description is given in S. R. Crockett's novel, *Lad's Love* (1897):

> A 'lane' is, in Galloway, a slow, untrouted, sullen, half-stagnant piece of water, loitering currentless across a meadow or peat-moor.

Latch – this term for a small stream flowing through boggy ground has a long history in Scots and dates back to the earliest stages of the language. Evidence for the word survives in Latin charters from the eleventh century. Place-names incorporating *latch* include Kirklatch near Pittenweem in Fife, Latchbrae in Edinburgh and Latch Burn in Perthshire.

Linn – also found in dialects in the north of England, *linn* 'waterfall' has been used to form place-names throughout Scotland. The Corra Linn Waterfalls on the River Clyde, Robert's Linn near Hawick and the Linn o' Dee are three striking examples. Descended from Old English *hlynn*, the term is recorded in a variety of Scottish texts dating back to the Middle Ages, including Alexander Montgomerie's poem *The Cherrie and the Slae* (c.1605):

> *The streame . . . growes ay broader nere the sea,*
> *Sen over the lin it came.*

Loch – perhaps the most characteristically Scottish word of all, *loch* is used throughout the country as the regular term equivalent to English 'lake'. The last two letters in *loch* are usually and traditionally pronounced like the -*ch* in *Bach*, but in parts of Scotland where the accent is becoming increasingly anglicised, the word sometimes sounds more like 'lock'. The term is Gaelic in origin, and travellers to Scotland will find lochs all over the countryside, from the famous Loch Ness with its legendary monster in the north, to the picturesque Loch Doon and Loch Dee in the south-west.

Mooth – often used to describe the outfall or lower end of a stream, river, estuary or inland sea, Scots *mooth* occurs in early place-names that pre-date the oldest Scots literature. The mouth of the Tweed is recorded as *Twedemud* around the year 1220, and as *Twedemouth* in 1337. Old documents can also show how place-names have evolved. In 1702, the *Records of the Convention of the Royal Burghs of Scotland* noted the 'Building of ane harbour in the moueth of Lossie', giving an insight into the history of the name of the Moray Firth harbour town now called Lossiemouth.

Plumb – used to describe a deep pool in a river or on the sea-bed, this term is found in a number of local names that rarely appear on official maps. George

Watson's *Roxburghshire Word-Book* (1923) mentions Jack's Plum and Pate's Plum, which may have been associated with local fishermen. An 1877 poem by William McHutchison, tells of fishing in 'Bailie's Plum' and a late eighteenth-century work entitled *Glasgow Past and Present* describes

> places in this part of the Clyde which went by the name of plumbs or holes, where several accidents have occurred.

Pot – often used to describe a deep hole or water-filled chasm in a river, a *pot* can also be a pool in rocks along the shoreline. The former type is often of particular relevance to anglers, as in William Sorley Brown's Selkirk tale, *The Ne'er-do-Weel* (1909):

> At the village of Ettrickbridge . . . there is a famed salmon pool or 'pot' known as the Loup.

There are many examples of the word in Old Scots, often in the context of changes in the condition of important rivers. *The Memorialls of the Trubles in Scotland and in*

England (c.1650) describes *the drying up of the pot of Brechin* and notes that *ane pot of the water of Brechin, callit Southesk, becam suddantlie dry.*

Pow – as a term found in the names of minor rivers and streams, *pow* is sometimes more narrowly defined as a slow-moving stream, or a natural or artificial ditch. This sense is perhaps most clearly reflected in some of the pows that border the Tay, the Forth and the Solway Firth. *Pow* is one of the most ubiquitous terms found in Scottish river-names. For example, the tributaries of the Nith include Cargen Pow and Drummillan Pow, and Pow Burn is a commonplace river-name found in many areas across Lowland Scotland including Ayrshire and Lothian.

Shon – in Shetland and Caithness, one of the words for a small loch or pool is *shon*, also used in the phrase *a shon of water* to indicate a temporary pool, or a water-filled pit. According to Jakob Jakobsen's *Etymological Dictionary of the Norn Language in Shetland* (1928–32), this term is frequently found in the names of small lakes, and could also be used of a swamp.

Stank – despite looking like a well-known past tense, this word has nothing necessarily to do with unpleasant odours. Derived from Old French *estanc*, 'stretch of (*stagnant*) shallow water', which becomes *étang* 'pond' in modern French, *stank* has several uses in modern Scots. It is perhaps best known as a Scots word for a drain or gutter (alongside other French-derived terms such as *cundie* and *syver*), but a stank can also be a pond, pool or swamp. There are several examples of field-names and minor names such as Stankhead, Stankend and Mill Stank containing this term, found across the country.

Stell – not recorded by the *Dictionary of the Scots Language* after 1900, a *stell* was a place where nets were drawn over a river to catch salmon. The names of several specific stells, in the parish of Dyke and Moy, in Elgin, appear in the *Statistical Account of Scotland* (1791–99):

Eth stell, Elven stell, the Sheriff's stell, and the Easter and Wester stells of Culbin.

Other examples can be found in modern field-names like Oldstell Plantation near the River Tweed.

Strind – a very small stream, or even a trickle of water or spilt liquid, may be described by this term. Some strinds are seasonal and only appear during particular weather conditions, such as heavy rains which cause the rivers to rise (or to be in spate, to use another useful Scottish term). *Strind* is also found in place-names in Orkney, Morayshire and Aberdeenshire.

Syke – also found in northern English dialects, *syke* denotes a small stream, rill or water-course, especially one that meanders through a hollow or across flat or boggy ground. Surviving place-names containing this term include Liggat Syke in West Lothian, Peat Syke in Ayrshire and Gogarloch Syke in Edinburgh. Sometimes modern names (particularly street-names) no longer have an obvious geographical connection to a small river, although indicating the historical presence of one.

Vatn – this term occurs in Shetland and is derived from Old Norse *vatn*. It can denote either water or a lake and is frequently used to form place-names including the old name *Sandvatn* (now Sandwater) in Shetland and Watten in Caithness. The replacement of *vatn* by *water* occurs quite frequently in such place-names; another example is the name Helga Water, near Hillswick in Shetland, formerly *Helgavatn*.

Watter – Scots have been using the word *watter* for many hundreds of years — at least since the medieval makar Robert Henryson described the *Twa Mice* drinking *watter cleir, In steid off wyne* in the late fifteenth century. Although not always reflected in the printed names recorded in gazetteers and street-maps, which are often standardised following English spelling, *watter* is frequently used in the names of rivers. A well-known example is the Water of Leith in Edinburgh; others include the Water of Aven in Aberdeenshire and the Water of Malzie in Wigtownshire.

Weel – a weel is a deep pool or whirlpool in a river or stream. In its description of the River Ayr in Ayrshire, the *Statistical Account of Scotland* (1834–45) reported that

> There has been a considerable loss of life in the
> Ayr, owing to the darkness of its waters concealing
> from the view of persons who had ventured into
> it, deep places, with which the river abounds,
> termed . . . 'Weels', almost every 'Weel' bearing the
> name of some person who has perished in it.

Other weels include Weel Pool and Barmuck Weel, both in Ayrshire.

The large number of Scots terms for different types of rivers and streams (and the obstacles you might encounter in them) reminds us of the importance that such landscape features had in days gone by. The traveller, the boatman or the fisherman all needed to know how to navigate their way through the pows and burns, latches and pots they might encounter. The history of some of these terms conjures picturesque images of Scotland's landscape, while others give us a sense of the ways in which former generations lived and worked.

3 Forests and Glens

The terms discussed in this chapter reflect the significant influence of Gaelic and Old Norse on Scots. Some also remind us of the traps that can culturally derail the unwary traveller. In much the same way that Americans typically walk around in public wearing *pants* and *suspenders* — while Brits tend to keep such things concealed — not everything is as it might seem at first sight. If a tree falls in a Scottish *forest,* is it a forest?

Carse – this word for a stretch of low alluvial land along the banks of a river is attested comparatively rarely in historical texts. James Robertson's *General View of the Agriculture in the Southern Districts of the County of Perth* (1794) informs us that:

> *The moss lies upon a field of clay, . . . a*
> *continuation of those rich, extensive flats in the*
> *neighbourhood of Falkirk and Stirling, distinguished*
> *by the name of carses.*

Although rare in literary use, *carse* is often found in place-names, as in the Carse of Gowrie, along the north shore of the Firth of Tay, and the Carse of Lecropt, near Bridge of Allan in Stirlingshire. The Carse of Stirling (or Carse of Tay) covers an area of nearly 40 square miles and is the largest of Scotland's flood plains.

Corrie – describing a hollow in a hill-side, or a hollow between hills or mountains, *corrie* has been recorded in Scots sources since the Middle Ages. It is derived from Gaelic *coire*, which can denote a cauldron, a whirlpool, or a hollow in a hill, and is found in place-names coined by Gaelic speakers. Examples include Coire an t-Sneachda in the Cairngorms, translated as *Corrie of the Snows*. Scots coinages are typically those of the type *Corrie of X*. where *corrie* is been added to an earlier name, as in Corrie of Bellaty in Angus.

Dean – a *dean* is a deep glen or valley, sometimes wooded, and often with a river running through it. Dean Village, in Edinburgh, where the land slopes down steeply to the Water of Leith, is one example. The old parish of Hassendean, in Roxburgh also takes its name from one such glen. In origin, the term derives from Old English *denu* 'valley', and is found in place-names in both Scotland and England. The place-name term **den** is closely related to the word *dean*.

Deel – also found with the spelling *dale*, as in English, this term is derived from Old English *dæl* and its Old Norse cousin *dalr*, which both mean 'valley'. In Shetland, the word is usually *dale*, but sometimes it becomes *daal,* as in the compound *daalamist, mist which gathers in valleys or on low-lying water, usually appearing at night and disappearing when the sun rises.* Names containing *dale,* such as Lauderdale and Teviotdale in the Borders, can refer to wide areas of land bordering rivers.

Den – related to the term **dean,** this is used in place-names to describe a deep hollow between hills. It occurs throughout Scotland, for example in Easter Denhead in Perthshire, Dura Den in Fife and Hawthornden in Midlothian. Dens can also be wooded, and the following quotation from Sir Walter Scott's novel, *Redgauntlet* (1824), shows the survival of this meaning in literary usage:

> *At length, our course was crossed by a deep dell or dingle, such as they call in some parts of Scotland a den, and in others a cleuch, or narrow glen. It seemed . . . steep, precipitous, and full of trees.*

The word was probably influenced by another meaning of den, *an animal's lair,* first recorded in Scots in Robert Henryson's fifteenth-century tale, *The Preaching of the Swallow*:

> *All wyld bestis . . . Drawis for dreid unto thair*
> *dennis deip.*

Forest – oddly enough, a Scottish forest does not necessarily contain a large number of trees. Since the eighteenth century, the word has had a specific meaning in Scots Law, referring to a large tract of ground which is not necessarily wooded, and is commonly bare and mountainous. Such lands were originally reserved for the hunting of deer and belonged to the Crown. In his *Journal of a Tour to the Hebrides* (1773), James Boswell remarked that the Cuillin Hills of Skye

> *make part of a great range for deer, which, though*
> *entirely devoid of trees, is in these countries called*
> *a forest.*

He was not the only one to be surprised by this use of the term. A volume of the *History of the Berwickshire Naturalists' Club* (1872) recounts a similar tale:

> *An Englishman, new to the Highlands, passing through a northern deer forest, remarked to his native companion that he was surprised to see no trees there. "Trees!" said the Highlander, with undisguised contempt, "wha ever heard tell o' trees in a forest?"*

We should never underestimate the value of local knowledge.

Gill – a *gill* is usually a narrow valley with steep, rocky sides. The term is derived from Old Norse *gil*, with the same meaning, and many of the place-names incorporating this term may be Scandinavian coinages. *Gill* occurs frequently in names across Scotland and especially in the Northern Isles, where Scandinavian influence had a significant impact. Examples include Djupa Gill and Feetnies Gill in Shetland, Fiddlers Gill and Garrion Gill in Lanarkshire, and Jenny Noble's Gill in Langholm, Dumfriesshire.

Glack – this term for a ravine or hollow between two hills made an appearance in literary use in James Robertson's novel *The Testament of Gideon Mack* (2007), as the name of a dangerous stretch of road. Other examples include West Glacks in Aberdeenshire and The Glack in Inverness-shire. While some names include Scots *glack*, in others the term represents Gaelic *glac* 'hollow, valley', from which the Scots term originated.

Glen – an archetypically Scottish word, *glen* is derived from Gaelic *glenn*, *gleann*. Historical forms of some names containing *glen*, such as Rutherglen in Lanarkshire, are found as early as the twelfth century. Many of the most famous (and most picturesque) Scottish glens, particularly those located in the Highlands of Scotland, represent original Gaelic rather than later Scots coinages. Examples include Glen Coe, Glen Etive, Glen Nevis, Glen Spean and Glen Shee.

Grain – derived from Old Norse *grein*, this term can be used of a fork or division in the course of a river or valley. An example is found in the 1825 *Supplement* to John Jamieson's *Etymological Dictionary of the Scottish Language* (1808):

> *The branches of a valley at the upper end, where it divides into two; as, Lewinshope Grains.*

Lewinshope, located in Yarrow in the Borders, is itself a valley.

Hause – although this term is perhaps better known as a Scots word for the neck or throat, it can also refer to a narrow passage between hills, or the head of a pass. This is the meaning of *hause* in names such as Hause Burn in Dumfriesshire. In place-names in the Borders, and in the English Lake District, *hause* is used specifically as a name for a narrow ridge connecting two heights.

Holm – denoting a meadow, or stretch of low-lying land beside a river, *holm* is found in a variety of

Lowland names including Broomholm and Lyneholm in Dumfriesshire, and Gadgirth Holm and Millholm in Ayrshire. The word derives from Old Norse *hólmr*, which can mean either a meadow, as in these south-western names, or an islet, as is the case for many of the names incorporating *holm* in the Northern Isles.

Hope – in the place-names of southern Scotland and northern England, this term is often associated with small enclosed upland valleys or hollows amongst hills. It is represented in Dryhope in Selkirkshire and Hopehead Burn in Peebles and derives from the Old English word *hop*, with the same sense. Coastal names containing *hope* may instead be derived from Old Norse *hóp*, 'a small land-locked bay or inlet'.

Howe – in place-names this term indicates a hollow, or low-lying piece of ground, and is found in such names as Hopeless Howe in Wigtownshire, surely an apt title for a depression. More typical is the Aberdeenshire name Howe Moss, although in some cases *howe* denotes a wide area of land surrounded by hills, such as the Howe o' the Mearns, south of Stonehaven in Aberdeenshire.

Lea – while there are several meanings of the Scots word *lea*, it frequently occurs in place-names denoting a piece of fallow ground, a field of grass, or a meadow. It is also used in the more general sense *open uncultivated ground.* There are many instances of its use in Scottish place-names across the Lowlands, including Woodhouselee in Midlothian, Torwoodlee in the Borders and Netherley in Aberdeenshire.

Muir – both Scots *muir* and English *moor* are descended from the Old English word *mōr*, which could originally denote both marshland and uncultivated ground. The Scots word has had various meanings over time, and in place-names it typically refers to moorland or uncultivated land. In the past, muirs could be held as part of an estate or could belong collectively to a local community. Many names include this term and there are many instances of the same name appearing in different parts of the country. Muirhead occurs in Angus, Fife, Lanarkshire and Ayrshire; Grangemuir in Fife and Ayrshire; and Muirhouses in Perth, Angus and Stirlingshire.

Park – in its earliest known use in Scots, a park was an enclosed area of land, often woodland or forest, where animals were kept for hunting. In later use the word developed other meanings including *meadowland, pasture land.* and *lands set aside for recreation.*

Place-names incorporating the term *park* often include terms for local plants or animals — there are several Broomparks and Deerparks. Also typical are names like Park End in Ayrshire and Park Foot in Stirlingshire, denoting the more southerly or lower end of a park, and there are Parkheads, denoting the northern or higher end of a park, in Aberdeenshire and Lanarkshire.

Peck – this word is not usually associated with rivers but, in local use in Dumfriesshire, it is figuratively applied to the great hollow shaped like a peck measure, from which the River Annan rises, also known as the Devil's Beef-tub. A reference to this use of the name can be found in the *Statistical Account of Scotland* for Dumfriesshire (1791–99):

> The spring of the Annan, . . . called the 'Annan
> Peck', or the Marquis of Annandale's 'Beef
> Stand'.

Qwaw – Eildon Quaw in the Borders and Castle Quaw near Cartland Crags in Lanarkshire both incorporate the term *qwaw*, which indicates a piece of very soft ground or quagmire. S. R. Crockett provides the following description in his novel, *The Raiders* (1894):

> Green, deceitful, 'quakkin-qua's,' covered with a
> scum that looked like tender young grass, but
> in which, at the first step, one might sink to the
> neck.

Reesk – place-names such as The Reesk and Reisk in Aberdeenshire, and Reisk near Kirriemuir in Angus indicate an area of untilled moor or marshy ground covered with natural grasses. Derived from Gaelic *riasg* 'sedge-grass', the word is attested in a variety of Scottish sources, from medieval Latin charters to twentieth-century Aberdeenshire poetry. In 1765, the *Records of the Town Council of Rothesay* noted:

> *A Riask or piece of Whinny ground* [i.e. ground covered in whins] *near to the Houses of Townhead.*

Shaw – denoting a small wood, especially one that grows naturally, or without cultivation, this term occasionally appears in literary texts, but is otherwise rarely used. There are many examples of *shaw* in place-names, including Wishaw in Lanarkshire, Stanley Shaw near Paisley and Pollokshaws in Glasgow, sometimes abbreviated as The Shaws. The word derives from Old English *sceaga* 'thicket, small wood'.

Shiel – although in modern use this word usually denotes a (temporary) hut or shelter used by shepherds in high or remote areas of pasture land, in Old Scots it could also refer to the pasture land itself, where sheep and cattle were traditionally driven in summer. Both meanings are reflected in place-names, where the word often occurs in the plural, and is sometimes spelled *shield*. Examples include Shiels in Aberdeen, Mid Foulshiels in West Lothian and Shields Rig in Lanarkshire.

Shieling – like **shiel**, this term can refer to either a shelter used by shepherds in high or remote areas of pasture land, or the pasture land itself. Both meanings were still in use until the twentieth century and shielings were often mentioned in charters, especially in the lists of the parts of an estate. Names containing this term include Shieling Burn in Argyllshire and Shieling Rig in Dumfriesshire.

Sink – a *sink* is, rather unsurprisingly, used of a low-lying area of land where water collects. Such areas are often marshy and treacherous. Although originally a Scots usage, this definition is current in US English. Michael Montgomery notes a similar definition, *a low-lying area or basin of land, usually having sunken ground,* in his *Dictionary of Smoky Mountain English* (2004), adding that the term also appears in place-names such as White Oak Sink in Tennessee. Until at least the late nineteenth century, the term was also used in Scots to refer to a coal-pit, or the shaft of a coal-mine. In some instances, coal-pits and boggy land go together. In *A General View of the Agriculture of the Counties of Kinross and Clackmannan* (1814), Patrick Graham comments on the sinks that are

> *small pits of eight or nine feet in diameter, and six or seven feet deep; they are to be met with frequently in this county. They are occasioned by the subsidence of the upper stratum, in fields perforated in every direction by coal-pits.*

Slack – this is thought to be derived from Old Norse *slakki*, 'a hollow between hills', but some meanings of the word may show influence from Scots **slock** and its ancestor, Gaelic *sloc*, 'a pit, a den'.

Examples include Slackend in West Lothian and Gateslack in Dumfriesshire. In modern use, and in minor names and field-names, a *slack* can also be a low-lying waterlogged depression in the ground, typically a marsh or morass. Sir Walter Scott notes this usage in his novel, *Guy Mannering* (1815):

> Between the farm-house and the hill-pasture was a
> deep morass, termed . . . a slack.

Slap – in place-names, a *slap* usually has nothing to do with violence, and instead refers to either a pass through hills, or a shallow valley. A particularly good example of the former sense is found in the name of Cauldstane Slap, a pass that lies between West and East Cairn Hills, and stretches from the Scottish Borders to West Lothian. The term is also sometimes spelled *slop*, as in the lost place-name *Barkerland Slop* (1707), noted in the *Dictionary of the Scots Language*. Such spellings are closer to the original Middle Dutch *slop* and Middle Low German *slop* from which the Scots word derives.

Slock – like a **slack**, a *slock* generally denotes a hollow between hills, or a pass, when it appears in place-names, though it can also indicate an inlet of the sea. Derived from Gaelic *sloc* 'pit, den' it is found in written sources from all over Scotland, including S. R. Crockett's account of the *hollow-throated pass . . . (with) the grim name of the Wolf's Slock,* in his southern Scottish novel, *The Raiders* (1893). A more northerly illustration is provided in the *Statistical Account of Scotland* for Aberdeenshire (1834–45), which describes the discovery of an old eyrie in *the slocks of Glencarvy.*

Strath – found in the names of large districts such as Strathclyde, Strathearn and Strathnaver, as well as more minor names such as Green Strath in Aberdeenshire and Helshetter Strath in Caithness, a *strath* is a wide river valley. The word is derived from Gaelic *srath*, and its frequent use in place-names reminds us of the former dominance of Gaelic across the country in medieval times.

Wham – as a place-name term, *wham* typically occurs in the south of Scotland, and denotes a little glen, or a broad hollow among hills through which a stream runs. The word has no connection with English *wham*, but derives from Old Norse *hvammr*, 'short valley, hollow'. The *Caledonian Mercury* (1773) discussed

> *The Growth of Young Planting, growing on that Brae called the Sandy Wham . . . on the North Esk.*

The diversity of words found across the country and across time attests to a complex network of terminology, some of which is now only known to us from place-names. It also provides some interesting fodder for riddles – where else but in Scotland can you encounter whams and slaps (and even a peck) while touring the countryside, yet still come home unscathed?

4 Sea and Coast

In this chapter, you will probably detect something of a bias towards Old Norse, especially in the sections on words from Insular Scots, the Scots of Orkney and Shetland. This is not the result of a Viking twisting my arm during the editorial process, but simply reflects the impact that the sea has had on the language of these communities over the centuries.

Bank – in Old Scots the term *sea-bank* was used to refer to the coast or sea-shore, as attested by the many Seabank Roads in Scotland's coastal towns and cities.

A *ank*, in place-names, is usually an edge of some kind, and the many Bankheads and Bankends typically refer to river-banks. *Bank* names often contain the names of local plants – in Sauchiebank in Edinburgh, *sauchie* means 'willowy, growing with willows'.

Cleugh – also sometimes spelled *cleuch*, this word can refer to either a cliff or a ravine with steep rocky sides. It is found in many place-names, often in conjunction with the name of a bird known to frequent such an area. In Berwickshire, for example, Earnscleuch contains the Scots term *earn* 'eagle', and Corbie Cleuch in Dumfriesshire contains Scots *corbie* 'crow'. With modified pronunciation, *cleuch* is also found in the place-name Buccleuch in Selkirk, famous for its Dukes and Border chieftains.

Drong – found in the Northen Isles, and derived from the Old Norse word *drangr*, 'a detached pillar of rock', this term is used in place-names, often in the plural, to denote high rock formations rising from the sea. The *Statistical*

Account of Scotland for Shetland (1834–45) notes *many curious rocks, the most remarkable ... situated at the back of Hillswick Ness, and called the Drongs.*

Eid – also found in the Northern Isles and derived from Old Norse, this term may be used either for an isthmus or a narrow neck of land jutting out into the sea. It can also refer to a sandbank cast up across the head of a bay. Jakob Jakobsen's *Etymological Dictionary of the Norn Language in Shetland* (1928–32) explains that in place-names *eid* is quite often compounded with Old Norse *mæf* 'slender', giving rise to forms such as *Mæfeid* or *Mæveid*, as found early, spell in the parish-name Northmavine.

Firth – derived from an Old Norse word related to *fjord*, this word describes an estuary or wide inlet of the sea. In historical documents it often appears in the form *frith*, which looks like an error to our modern eyes but is a reminder that not all forms of language (including modern Scots) are standardised. A seventeenth-century example occurs in Robert Bell's account of the *Siege of the Castle of Edinburgh* (1689) – witnesses reported seeing *a fleet of Dutch doggers (ships) making up the Frith*.

In place-names, *frith* sometimes refers to a wood, or a clearing in a wood, but in such cases we are dealing with a completely different word, derived from Old English. Fortunately the local topography can often help to determine which of the terms has been used.

Flow – the best-known Scottish name including this term is Scapa Flow in the Orkney Islands, which played an important strategic role in the First and Second World Wars. A *flow* is an arm of the sea, or a bight, channel or haven with deep water or strong flowing tides. The *Dictionary of the Scots Language* records use of the word with reference to the Pentland Firth in the mid-twentieth century. Inland, the term usually refers instead to a morass, swamp or peat-bog.

Geo – frequently found in place-names in Caithness and the Northern Isles, a *geo* is as an inlet of the sea. It derives from Old Norse *gjá* 'cleft, chasm', and in Orkney often indicates a ravine. Names including this term are frequently located in places with a dramatic and rugged coastline, as at Wife Geo in Caithness, Sultigeo in Orkney and Calder's Geo in Shetland.

Gloup – the sound of this word seems particularly appropriate for the name of a watery place, and in the far north of Scotland and the Northern Isles it denotes a sea-cave or chasm. In *The Orkney Norn* (1929), Hugh Marwick notes that the term is used specifically to refer to

> a deep chasm or pit a little way back from the cliff-edge, but having an opening to, or connexion with, the sea down below. Looking down into the gloop one may see the sea dashing about in the bottom. A gloop is thus a big cave, the top of which has fallen in at the inner end.

Gloups can have supernatural connections, as in Robert Menzies Fergusson's *Rambling Sketches in the Far North* (1884):

> *This idea [that the elves were melancholy] probably originated from the moaning sound made by the wind and waves in the geos and gloups where they were supposed to dwell.*

Hause – this Scots word for the neck is sometimes figuratively applied to a narrow water-channel. In *The Orkney Norn* (1929), Hugh Marwick noted the diminutive variant Hassie as a name for *a narrow neck of water between Thieves-holm and the shore*, **holm** being a term for a small island in the Scots of the Northern Isles. In other contexts it is used of narrow valleys, or narrow ridges connecting two heights.

Holm – although used throughout the country in names denoting meadowland or low-lying land beside a river, as in Broomholm and Langholm in Dumfriesshire, this term has a different application in the Northern Isles. In Orkney and Shetland, *holm* more usually denotes a small grassy island in a loch or off the coast of the larger islands. These small islets are generally uninhabited and used as pasturage for sheep. Examples include Muckle Green Holm in Orkney and Lady's Holm in Shetland.

Hope – in coastal names, such as St Margaret's Hope in Orkney, *hope* generally indicates a small land-locked bay or inlet, and is derived from Old Norse *hóp*.

Inch – this term derives from Gaelic *innis*, which in place-names typically denotes either an island, or meadowland beside a river. These same meanings have been borrowed into Scots and several names containing this term can be found close to major rivers, such as Whiteinch and Abbot's Inch on the banks of the River Clyde. When combined with a Gaelic term, as in Inch Garvie in the Firth of Forth, it is likely to indicate an original Gaelic coinage. Gaelic names usually reflect the typical noun-adjective word order characteristic of Celtic languages, whereas in Scots, as in English, the regular word order dictates that nouns follow adjectives.

Kyle – derived from Gaelic *caol* 'narrow', *kyle* denotes a narrow strait of water. Well-known examples include Kyle of Lochalsh, Kyle of Sutherland and the Kyles of Bute. The word has been recorded in Scots sources since the sixteenth century, one of the first being Donald Munro's *Western Isles of Scotland and genealogies of the clans* (1549):

> Ane ile . . . with ane richt dangerous kyle & stream.

Lair – low-lying, muddy land may be described as a *lair*, and the word is attested with this meaning in Scots texts dating back to the seventeenth century. An entry in the *Account Book of Sir John Foulis* from 1693 provides a descriptive illustration, when

> 4 souldiers helped the coatch [coach] out of the lair beyond the Coltbridge.

The term is Scandinavian in origin, and derives from Old Norse *leir* 'mud', which was used to coin Lerwick in Shetland, literally (if not poetically) meaning 'mud bay'.

Links – no visitor to Scotland with an interest in golf can fail to be unaware of the word *links*, which refers to sandy coastal strips, covered with turf, grass and gorse. Place-names incorporating this term include the Links of Leith, Kirkcaldy Links, Lundin Links, the Links of Montrose, and Dornoch Links. Links golf courses are found in several areas of Scotland, notably in the south-west and the north-east. The association of links with golf has led to the term being applied to some golf courses not located by the sea, such as Bruntsfield Links in Edinburgh.

Machair – this term, derived from Gaelic *machair*, refers to a stretch of low-lying land by the sea, often covered with natural grasses and used for rough grazing. In Galloway, it is used specifically of the lands bordering the Solway Firth or Luce Bay. That said, about half of all

Scottish machair land is found in the Outer Hebrides. It is particularly fertile ground and is home to many species of birds and rare flowers.

Merse – this is flat and often marshy land, bordering a river, an estuary or the sea, and is specifically applied to the (partly reclaimed) land bordering the Solway in the south-west. An interesting point of information was recorded by the *Dumfries and Galloway Standard* regarding these lands, in 1954:

> *In response to inquiries concerning the public rights on the Merseland . . . it is considered necessary to draw attention to the fact that the Caerlaverock merselands, which comprise those extensive areas of grazing land bordering the Solway Shore between the mouths of the rivers Nith and Lochar and which are marked on the Ordnance Survey Maps as 'Merse' and 'Saltings', are the private property of his Grace the Duke of Norfolk.*

Mussel – the town of Musselburgh in Midlothian takes

its name from the nearby mussel beds and is first recorded in charters dating from the eleventh century. Mussel Bed in Ross-shire and Mussel Craig in Aberdeenshire provide further examples of the use of the term in place-names, although in Mussel Craig the term may refer to the shape of the *craig* or hill, rather than its actual proximity to molluscs.

Oyce – mainly found in Orkney, this word of Scandinavian origin denotes an inlet of the sea that may be cut off by a bar of shingle. The *Dictionary of the Scots Language* notes that the diminutive form Ossag was used to describe the mouth of the Thurso River by a local 'informant' (a dictionary spy) in 1964.

Scaup – also found in the form *scalp*, this term is used to describe a bank of shellfish, especially mussels or oysters, sometimes appearing in local, minor names. An article in the *Montrose Chronicle* from 1821 noted that 'the Muscle Scalps and White Fish Bait, on the Sands of Dun' were to be rented, and in 1965 the *Scots Magazine* commented on their gradual disappearance:

> Scalps in the Forth died out about 1920, and those
> in the Orkneys, Outer Hebrides, many West Coast
> lochs, and Luce Bay, also disappeared, possibly
> because of hard indiscriminate fishing without care
> for breeding oysters.

Shauld – areas in rivers or the sea where the water is not deep are sometimes known as *shaulds* in Scots. Both Scots *shauld* and English *shoal* are derived from the Old English adjective *sceald*, 'shallow'.

In Samuel Hibbert's *A Description of the Shetland Islands* (1822), mention is made of a song

> named the Shaalds of Foula, bearing allusion to a
> profitable fishery for cod that was long conducted
> upon those shaalds or shoals.

Although not widespread throughout Scotland, the word was recorded in use in Shetland, Orkney, Fife and Ayr in 1970 (see the *Dictionary of the Scots Language*).

Skerrie – these are isolated rocks or islets in the sea, often covered at high tide. When used in the plural, *skerries*, the word refers to a chain of rocks, or a reef. It occurs in such names as Oot Skerries and Ve Skerries in Shetland. The Scottish ballad, *The Great Silkie of Sule Skerrie*, provides a cautionary tale about the creatures that may be encountered in Scotland's coastal waters. The eponymous hero is 'a man, upo the lan, An . . . a silkie in the sea'. Maids should be wary of this half-man, half-seal, who might leave them with a supernatural bairn if they give in to his charms.

Sound – several inlets of the sea and narrow channels of water around Scotland have specific names in which this term is combined with another place-name or island-name. In the north-west of Scotland, for example, between the Ardnish and Ardnamurchan peninsulas, you will find the Sound of Arisaig, recently designated a marine Special Area of Conservation. The island of Raasay is separated from Skye by the Sound of Raasay, and the Sound of Rum lies between the islands of Rum and Eigg. The Sounds of Eigg and Muck largely exist to inspire quips from punning tourists.

Strand – sometimes this term refers to a river, but it can also denote the land bordering a river or the sea. Literary uses of *strand* date back to the Middle Ages, and include William Dunbar's poetic description of 'schip-wrichtis (ship-builders), hewand (cutting wood) upone the strand'. In Robert Burns' poem (and song), *It Was A' For Our Rightfu' King*, it is clear that he is referring to the coast, when he writes 'We left fair Scotland's strand'. Minor names and street-names of coastal areas often incorporate this term, such as North and South Strand Street in Stranraer.

Voe – in place names, this term is sometimes represented as *Waa* or (when preceded by another term) *-wall*, although it also appears in its more regular form, as in Sullom Voe, Orka Voe and West Voe in Shetland. The word derives from Old Norse *vágr* 'bay, sea inlet' and denotes an inlet of the sea or a deep bay or long creek. It is frequently found in place-names in the Northern Isles.

Wick – place-names incorporating the term *wick* usually derive from one of two sources. Some reflect use of the Old English word *wīc* '(dependent) farm', as in Hedderwick 'heather farm' in Angus and Fishwick 'fish farm' in Berwickshire, while others, such as Lerwick in Shetland and Wick in Caithness, derive from Old Norse *vík* 'bay'. In *A Vertebrate Fauna of the Shetland Islands* (1899), Arthur Evans and Thomas Buckley remarked that the various inlets of the sea

> *are variously styled Wick, Voe, or Geo, according to their breadth and the nature of their surroundings.*

The Vikings did not only settle in Shetland. They also had a significant linguistic impact on the Gaelic of the Western Isles, and Anglo-Scandinavian settlers who moved into the south of Scotland from England added many Norse words to the Scots language. The similarity of terms derived from Old Norse and Old English can often be confusing, and many an inquirer has ended up with their wicks in a twist. Particularly difficult are names like Prestwick, which seem most likely to be Old English *wīc* 'farm', yet are situated in a bay on the coast.

5 Buildings and Settlements

Some of the terms in this chapter remind us that although Scots shares many words with English, many of these words are used slightly differently north and south of the Border. You may be surprised to see some of the following terms described as 'Scots', because they are also perfectly regular in Scottish English. In many ways it is difficult to draw a line between th two, and many modern commentators choose not to, instead describing Scots as a linguistic continuum that reaches from Broad Scots to Scottish Standard English.

Academy – in Scotland, the word *academy* may be used in several different contexts, but in relation to public buildings it often denotes a school for higher secondary education (i.e. for young people from the ages of 11/12 to 17/18), generally set up in a burgh by the local authority. The term was derived from the English Dissenting Academies of the 18th century, run on similar lines. In Scotland the word may now be applied to any state secondary school. Very often it is also part of the formal title of the institution, as in the names of Kilmarnock Academy, Belmont Academy and Prestwick Academy in Ayrshire.

Bastile – often found in the form *bastle*, this term for a strong stone tower or fortress occurs in such names as Bastleridge and Kelloe Bastle in Berwickshire and is derived from Old French *bastile* 'a building'. As noted by the *Statistical Account of Scotland* for Berwickshire (1791–99),

The last mentioned vestige of feudal antiquity

was that of the bastiles . . . These edifices not only
served the purposes of prisons, but . . . constituted
a chain of fortresses, running . . . from almost the
one end of the county to the other.

Biggin – this is a Scots word for a building, derived
from Scots *bigg*, meaning 'to build', from the Old Norse
verb *byggja*, 'inhabit, dwell in, build'.

Places called Newbiggin or Newbigging can be found in
many counties including Angus, Lanarkshire and Orkney.
The word *bigg* is also used in a useful proverb, recorded
in Andrew Cheviot's *Proverbs of Scotland* (1896):
If he's biggit in the moss, he maun gang into the
mire the Scots equivalent of the man who built his
house on sand.

Bothy – while this term may be used of any basic
dwelling or shelter, it can also refer to some form of
(temporary) living quarters for workmen, or a shelter
on a hillside for shepherds, climbers or hill-walkers.

Historically, it was also used of an independent building on a farm, used to house unmarried male farm servants. In his book on Glaswegian dialect, *The Patter* (1985), Michael Munro notes that a *bothy* can be *a labourer's shelter on a building site* or a *sophisticated portakabin*.

Broch – if you are travelling around Scotland, particularly in the Northern and Western Isles, you are likely to encounter one of the prehistoric round towers known as brochs. Especially well-preserved examples can be seen, dominating the skyline, on the Island of Mousa in Shetland and at Dun Carloway on the Isle of Lewis. There are around 500 known brochs in Scotland, though many are badly ruined.

Bucht – in place-names, it is often difficult to distinguish the term *bught*, 'a sheep-fold', from *bught*, 'a bend', although sometimes the context provides a clue. In the case of the Kirkcudbrightshire name Sheep Bught Rock, for example, we can be fairly certain that there is or was a sheep-fold at this location. In the Borders you will find such names as Buchtrig and Bucht Sike, in Lanarkshire, Bucht Slack, and in Ayrshire, Bucht Burn.

Burgh – historically, a burgh (rhymes with *thorough*) was a town with special privileges, conferred by royal charter. Some of the oldest burghs are Edinburgh, Elgin, Perth, Roxburgh and Stirling, all of which were established as burghs by the mid-twelfth century. The word is derived from Old English *burg* and Scottish names incorporating this term typically date back to the Old English period, before the year 1100.

But-n-Ben – this is one of the words that has become associated with the romantic view of traditional Scotland, as it refers to the old-style dwelling made up of two rooms, the *but* and the *ben*. The but is the kitchen or outer room, while the ben is the 'good' room, the inner room. The association of the but-n-ben with couthy Scottish culture was very effectively turned on its head in Matthew Fitt's recent science fiction novel, *But n Ben A-Go-Go* (2000).

Clachan – this term was adopted into Scots from Gaelic *clachan* 'a village with a church'. Many places around Scotland took their name directly from the Gaelic word, such as Clachan on the Isle of Lismore, Clachan in the north of the Isle of Skye, and Clachan in Caithness. In Old Scots, clachans are often mentioned in legal documents. For example, the *Muniments of the Royal Burgh of Irvine* (1608) stipulates that people could be fined for the keeping of

> *liquere* [alcohol] *in ony clachan.*

The word also appears in modern Scots literature, including Anna Blair's novel, *The Rowan on the Ridge* (1980):

> *They sailed past creeks and fisher clachans where beachcombers and bairns waved them by.*

Cot – generally denoting a small, humble house or shelter, though sometimes also used in Old Scots of a sheep-fold, this word derives from Old English *cot* and its Old Norse cousin *kot*. The *Statistical Account of Scotland* for Roxburgh (1791–9) noted that

> *Eleven or twelve* [farmers] *in the village of Roxburgh are called cotlanders, possessing from his Grace the Duke of Roxburgh about two acres of land each, together with a house, yard, and liberty of pasturing their cows in an adjacent loaning.*

Place-names incorporating the term occur frequently across the country, and include Sheepcot Hill near Dumfries, Washingcot Rocks in Morayshire and Cotmuir in West Lothian.

Croft – a characteristically Scottish word, particularly associated with the Highlands and Western Isles, *croft* derives from Old English and denotes a smallholding. In modern Scotland, the term is used of specific agricultural units, protected by special legislation since the late nineteenth century. In Scots place-names, *croft* may combine with terms relating to size, as in Longcroft in Stirlingshire, or with occupational terms, as in Friars

Croft in West Lothian and the lost name Beadsmans Croft in Edinburgh.

Doocot – also known as *dookets*, doocots are the Scots equivalent of English dove-cots, showing the characteristic loss of -v- that you will also encounter in such Scots words as *siller* 'silver, money', *hae* 'have', *gie* 'give' and *loe* 'love'. In modern Scots a doocot is also a pigeonhole. Not so long ago I overheard someone paraphrasing dooket as 'wee box' in a formal business setting. Local knowledge can be very useful.

Fank – this term for an enclosure for farm animals derives from Gaelic *fang* and occurs in minor names such as Fank Wood in Argyll and Fank Burn in Perthshire. It was sometimes used of cattle-fairs, which were usually held near such enclosures, as attested by the *Statistical Account of Scotland* for Argyllshire (1834–45):

Formerly there were several small fairs, called Fanks in the parish [of Ardnamurchan].

Grange – in Old Scots, a grange could be either a barn or store-house for grain, or a farming establishment (often belonging to a religious house or a feudal lord) with granaries for storing crops. Sir Walter Scott's novel, *The Antiquary* (1816), makes reference to this meaning of the word, in the description of

> *a grange, or solitary farm-house, inhabited by the bailiff, or steward, of the monastery.*

The term was borrowed from Old French and is first recorded in Scots sources from the fifteenth century. It often occurs in place-names in combination with a pre-existing name, as in Grange of Conon in Angus, Grange of Lindores in Fife, and Grange of Cree in Wigtownshire.

Hame – like **toun**, this is one of the many words that has undergone only minor changes during its evolution from Old English to modern Scots. Hame is derived from Old English *hām*, which could denote a village, estate or dwelling. Some of the Scottish names that incorporate this term are in fact Old English coinages. For example, the names Birgham and Edrom in Berwickshire are both recorded in charters that pre-date the 'beginning' of Scots in the year 1100 (*Brygham, Bricgham* 1095, *Ederham* 1095). Names recorded later, like Caldhame in West Lothian are probably Scots coinages, though some names were established long before they were written down.

Hoose – the ancestor of Scots *hoose* is Old English *hūs*, and like **hame** and **toun** this is yet another example of a Scots word that retains much of its original Old English character. In England, Old English *hūs* was affected by sound changes which gave rise to the modern form *house*, but the pronunciation of Scots *hoose* has remained very close to that of the Old English term. Northerly place-names that incorporate Scots *hoose* may instead show derivation from Old Norse *hús*, cousin to the Old English word. For instance, Shetland Scots *hoosamil, husamil*, meaning a road or space between houses, is of Old Norse origin and can be compared to the Norwegian dialect word *husamillom* meaning *from one house to another.*

This is related to the phrase *to geng hoose-a-mila to go from house to house (gathering news or gossip).*

Howf – this term typically denotes a favourite haunt or meeting place, often a public house. However, *howf* is also used of a shelter or place of refuge, specifically a natural or improvised shelter used by mountaineers. According to an issue of the *Scottish Mountaineering Club Journal* from 1948,

> *The best known example of a mountain howff is the Shelter Stone of Loch Avon. Howf* can also denote *a shelter with a latrine used by workmen on a building site,* as recorded in the periodical *The Builder* (1952). In Dundee, *howf* (perhaps a different word) also indicates the burial-ground in the centre of the city which was originally the courtyard of the Greyfriars Monastery. This use of *howf,* meaning a churchyard or kirkyard, was also known

to local 'informants' (or dictionary spies) from Kincardineshire and Ayrshire, who helped provide information for the *Scottish National Dictionary* (1931–76).

Kirk – a very characteristic Scottish term in modern times, *kirk* is derived from Old Norse *kirkja* 'church'. During the Middle Ages, however, the word *kirk* was also found in many parts of England, as a result of the influence of the Danelaw, the area of north-east England that was under Danish rule during parts of the ninth and tenth centuries. A special set of place-names containing *kirk* are of particular historical interest because they reveal an intermixing of Celtic and Germanic cultures. In the case of Kirkcudbright, for example, *kirk* is combined with a form of the name of the English Saint *Cuthbert*, the place-name's structure following the word-order typical of Celtic languages like Gaelic. Had the typical Germanic word-order found in Scots, Old Norse and Old English been used instead, Kirkcudbright would probably have been named Cuthbert's Church or

Cuthbert's Kirk, with the qualifying term preceding the noun.

Lodge – besides its Masonic connections, there are a number of other Scottish contexts where *lodge* has a specific meaning. In mining circles it could refer to a pithead shelter, as described by Thomas Stewart in *Among the Miners* (1893):

> the lodge, that is, a little rude hut that no 'hill' was considered complete without in those days. Here, 'hill' is the pithead where the piles of hewn coal accumulate.

In the Highlands, a lodge might instead be a house used primarily to accommodate hunters during the shooting season.

Mains – this term for the home farm of an estate, cultivated for the proprietor, still occurs throughout Scotland as a farm name, taking the form '*Mains* of . . .' in northern Scotland and as '. . . *Mains*' in the rest of the country. Examples include Blackburn Mains and Carberry Mains in West Lothian, and Mains of Ardestie and Mains of Balgavies in Angus. The word is a shortened form of *demense* 'land possessed or occupied by the owner himself, and not held of him by any subordinate tenant', and was borrowed from Anglo-Norman.

Pendicle – generally speaking, a *pendicle* is something dependent on, or subordinate to, something else and in place-names it usually indicates a piece of land that originally formed part of a larger holding or farm. Some names undergo curious changes when their meaning ceases to be transparent. Pinnacle in Roxburgh seems to be one such name, recorded as *Pendickill* on a seventeenth-century map, but later re-interpreted. Pendicles would frequently be let to sub-tenants, who were known as *pendiclers*. The *Statistical Account of Scotland* for Dumfriesshire (1834–45) states that the lands comprising the Barony of Lochmaben, also known as the Fourtowns, were believed to have been

> *granted in small pendicles by King Robert*
> *Bruce . . . to the domestic servants.*

Shiel – this term was often used in place-names to denote a piece of pasturage on which a shepherd's hut was built, but it could also mean the hut itself. The same variation in meaning occurs for **shieling**. A dated but informative definition is given by William Gardiner in *The Flora of Forfarshire* (1848):

> *A shieling, or shiel, is a small rude hut or cottage,*
> *constructed for the accommodation of shepherds*
> *during the summer months they reside among the*
> *mountains. It is built of turf or rough stones, and*
> *generally thatched . . . the fire is lighted on the*
> *floor, and an opening in the roof, at one end of the*
> *dwelling, is deemed quite sufficient for the egress*
> *of the smoke.*

Shieling – like **shiel**, a shieling could be either a hut or shelter used by shepherds in high or remote areas of pasture land, or it could refer to the pasture land itself, where sheep and cattle were traditionally driven in summer. Shielings are often mentioned in charters, especially in the detailed lists of the components of an estate. In his autobiography of 1800, the Scottish church leader Alexander Carlyle recalled visiting one such shelter:

> *I was obliged to lodge in what they call a shieling, where I was used with great hospitality and uncommon politeness by a young farmer and his sister, who were then residing there, attending the milking of the ewes.*

Toun – like **hame**, this word has altered little in the course of its evolution from Old English *tūn*, which could denote either an enclosure, a dwelling or a village. In place-names, the term frequently combines with the name of a person, as in Edgarton in Dumfriesshire,

Johnston in Renfrewshire and Malcolmstone in Midlothian. Peterhead in Aberdeenshire is known as The Blue Toun and Langholm in Dumfriesshire is known as The Muckle Toun.

Unthank – in Old Scots, this word, meaning 'ingratitude' is recorded in a number of different sources, including William Stewart's account of England's Edward I in his *Buik of the Croniclis of Scotland* (1535):

> *Edward with the lang schankis / That efterwart did Scotland greit vnthankis.*

In the Lanarkshire names High Unthank and Laigh Unthank, as in similar names found in England, unthank denotes a place occupied without consent, sometimes described as a 'squatter farm'. Unthank is also the name of the imaginary city in Alasdair Gray's novel, *Lanark* (1981).

Scottish place-names, real and imaginary, often feature in literature and film, the latter being loosely based on the former. George Douglas Brown's 'Barbie', Lewis Grassic Gibbon's 'Blawearie', A. J. Cronin's 'Tannochbrae' and Dudley Watkins' 'Auchtershoogle' all have the power to influence the atmosphere of a story. The sounds, spellings and cultural associations of the names they mimic tell a complex story of Scotland's history and evolution.

6 Streets and Bridges

Friars Vennel

Most street-names were coined considerably later than the names of settlements and topographical features, and the process of naming new streets (and re-naming old streets) is an ongoing cultural activity. A recent example is Vettriano Vale, a new street in Levenvale, Fife, which was named after the Scottish painter Jack Vettriano in 2005. Renaming is often more contentious. Baker's Lane in St Andrews originally had the Scots name Baxter's Wynd, and this change (although historical) has often been seen as an unnecessary anglicisation.

Bow – in place-names, *bow* often indicates something shaped like an arch, and in street-names such as The Netherbow in Edinburgh it refers to the site of an arch that marked the entrance to the **burgh**. Bow Brigs, or arched bridges, are a common feature of the Scottish countryside, and this compound was used frequently in Old Scots. Sources quoted in the *Dictionary of the Scots Language* include an entry in the *Burgh Records for Peebles* (1653) on *the building of ane bow bridge over the miln-dam* and an entry in the *Burgh Records of Aberdeen* (1610), about the *bow brig . . . ower the Den Burne*.

Brae – although often used in place-names to denote a hill, in street-names *brae* can also indicate a road with a steep gradient. Examples include Windmill Brae in Aberdeen and Bouly Brae in Arbroath. In the eighteenth century, a *brae* could also be an artificial bank built across a river to trap salmon. A failing enterprise may be *gaein doon the brae*, but *set a stout hert tae a stey* [steep] *brae* to face adversity with resolve.

Brig – derived from Old Norse *bryggja*, *brig* is the cousin of English *bridge*, which derives from Old English *brycg*. A famous Scottish brig is the Brig o' Doon, which (unsurprisingly) crosses the river Doon in Ayrshire and is immortalised in Robert Burns' tale of *Tam o Shanter*. Unlike *Brigadoon*, tourists can visit it all year round.

Causey – denoting a street or pavement laid with cobble-stones (rather than flagstones or **plainstanes**), this word is recorded in Scots sources from the fifteenth century onwards. In Old Scots, causeys were the scenes of all manner of activities. The *Records of Elgin* (1599) report that a certain Johne Stewart was accused of

> *playing at the bowallis* [bowls] *on the calsaye the tyme of the evenyng prayeris*

and in the late sixteenth-century *Memorials of Transactions in Scotland*, there is an account of an incident in Edinburgh during which *bulletis rebowndis of (off) the calsey,* injuring Lord Fleming. Less dramatically, the *Register of the Privy Council of Scotland* (1628) notes the more practical information that 'William Parke . . . built upon the rivers Cader and Coven eache of thame a bridge with calseyes'.

Close – this word means different things to different people. In some parts of the country, mainly in Glasgow and the south-west, a *close* is the entry to a tenement house, the open passage-way giving access to the common stairs and the floors above. In other places, however, the word is more frequently understood to indicate either a narrow lane with houses on each side, or a passageway leading into a courtyard. This meaning is particularly evident in Edinburgh, especially in the names of the narrow streets and passages leading off the Royal Mile. These are often named after specific professions, individuals or local activities, and include Advocates' Close, Mary King's Close, Lady Stair's Close and Fleshmarket Close.

Court – as in English, a court is an enclosed area, but some uses of the word are specific to Scotland. The back-court, or back-courtie, refers to the garden or yard at the back of a tenement building. In *Row Laddie Sixty Years On* (1987), Norman Lynn recalls the games played in such places:

> *Football and cricket were discouraged in the*
> *confinement of the back-coorty, so Beezy, where*
> *the ball was struck with bare hand and less likely to*
> *cause damage, was substituted.*

Gate – this term is derived from Old Norse *gata* and denotes a way or road. It occurs frequently in street-names, including Glasgow's Trongate and Gallowgate, and Edinburgh's Canongate and Cowgate. Gate can also refer to a person's manner or style; if you *gang yer ain gate*, you go your own way. Historical sources reveal a number of other uses. The *Statistical Account of Scotland* for Clackmannanshire (1791–9) explains that

> *coal, when led to the shore of Alloa for exportation,*

pays a tax . . . to the family of Mar, called Gate Mail. It was originally demanded, for the liberty of exporting the coal from the Pow of Alloa, and because the road leading through the estate to the harbour was a private one, though used by the public.

Gushet – this is a triangular piece of land, especially one lying between two adjacent properties. It occurs in a variety of minor names including Gushetfaulds in Glasgow, and it appears in the title of Willam Alexander's Scots novel, *Johnny Gibb of Gushetneuk* (1884). A 'gushet house' was a building that stood on a corner, or created an angle between two roads. You might recognise the similarity of *gushet* and *gusset*. The English word was borrowed from Old French *gousset*, but the Scots form appears to be closer to a variant of this word, Old French *gouchet*.

høvi-brigg – A *høvi* is a fish-trap made of basket-work, typically used in trout-streams in Orkney and

Shetland. It is also found in the compound *høvi-brigg*, indicating a bridge to which such a trap is fastened. The *Statistical Account of Scotland* for Shetland (1834–45) provides the following description:

> *The houvie is . . . wide at the one end, and narrow at the other. A dike is built across the burn, leaving an open space in the middle sufficient to admit the wider end of the houvie. After the houvie is firmly placed in this open space, a person, with a stick in his hand, wades down the burn, and drives the trouts before him. Having entered the houvie and reached its narrow end, they cannot turn to get out again.*

Kirkstyle – also known as a kirkyard-style, this is a term for a gateway to a kirkyard (or churchyard) that has been recorded in use in Scots texts since fifteenth century. More specifically, it is typically a narrow entrance enclosed by bars, a wicket or an arrangement of steps, where meetings were arranged and announcements made, and where the bier was received into the church-yard at funerals. *Kirkstyle* is sometimes used as the name of a house or farm near the kirkyard.

Loan – before the enclosing of fields, a *loan* was a strip of grass of varying breadth that ran through arable farmland, often linking it with the common grazing ground of the community. This land served as a pasture, a driving road and a milking place for cattle, and as a common green. Names like Loanend and Loanheid indicate the extremities of a loan. This term also gave rise to the expression *loan-soup*, which was milk taken freshly from a cow and given to strangers who happened upon the loan at milking-time.

Mercat – the centre of a town mercat (or market) was marked in many Scottish towns with a wooden or stone cross. Some mercat crosses still survive, although now they are often historical monuments rather than a focal point for the community. Mercats could be arranged to serve all manner of different trades, and in medieval Scotland there were butter-mercats, cale-mercats (cabbage), clathe-mercats (cloth), corn-mercats, salt-mercats, timmer-mercats (timber), victuall-mercats and woll-mercats (wool). Many such markets have left their mark on local names, as for example the Grassmarket in Edinburgh.

Neuk – generally pronounced like the word *nuke*, though hopefully less dangerous, this term is used in Scots to denote a projecting corner of land. The most prominent such place-name is the East Neuk of Fife, but the term also occurs in street-names such as Craig Neuk Street in Motherwell and Wallneuk Street in Paisley. The word has been recorded in Scottish sources since the fourteenth century and sometimes refers to a remote part of an area of land. A late sixteenth-century work by John Hamilton, *Ane Catholik and Facile Traictise*, describes Scotland itself as

  ane nuke of the warld.

Neuks can also be hiding-places, but this quotation from James Robertson's novel, *The Fanatic* (2000), reminds us to protect our secrets:

When the bailies came to take them to prison,
they asked Thomas if he had any money to
secure . . . Jean piped up, and kindly showed them
all the panels and neuks where it was hidden.

Pend – in general, this term denotes the arch of a bridge or gateway, and sometimes refers to a vaulted gateway, such as can be seen at the entrance to the Abbeys of St Andrews and Arbroath. In street-names, however, it is most often used of a vaulted or arched passageway, especially one that leads from the street into the back-**court** of a block of houses. Examples include Bucclech Pend and Porteous Pend in Edinburgh. This term also lies behind the derivation of *Pen' Folk*, a short-lived religious sect with Baptist principles which formed in the late eighteenth-century and met in a pend (or *pen*, as it is sometimes known) in the High Street in Paisley.

Plainstanes – as opposed to a **causey**, which is paved with cobblestones, a road or pavement might be paved with flagstones or plainstanes. The word is sometimes used to indicate a paved side-walk or pavement, as in the following quotation from J. G. Lockhart's *Memoirs of the Life of Sir Walter Scott* (1815):

> *Better walking on the beach at Worthing than on the plainstanes of Prince's Street, for the weather is very severe here indeed.*

A plainstane could also be a paved area, often the main square of a town. The spelling plainstone also exists, but the use of the word in any form is largely restricted to Scotland.

Raw – this term for a row of houses, generally of a uniform construction with common gables, is frequently found in the names of streets. Some names which were initially spelled this way have been altered to *row* as a result of anglicisation. Shiprow in Aberdeen, for instance, is recorded in medieval documents as *Schipraw* (1417), and Potterow in Edinburgh is *Potter raw* in sixteenth-century sources. The town of Huntly in Aberdeenshire used to be known as *the raws of Strathbogie*.

The origin and meaning of the street-name Rotten Row, found in several towns in Scotland and England, has yet to be explained satisfactorily. Various suggestions have been made for the first part of the name, including the ideas that it relates to either a place that is rat-infested, or was intended to mean 'the king's road' from French *route du roi*, but so far opinion remains divided, and the true solution may not yet have been identified.

Sheuch – also spelled *sheugh*, this term can denote a gutter in a street, or a ditch or drain, though in street-names it more commonly refers to a narrow lane between houses. The *-ch* or *-gh* at the end of the word is pronounced like the *-ch* in *loch* (rather like the *-ch* in Bach), but despite the guttural delights of its pronunciation, some of the streets that were once known as sheuchs have since been given alternative names. For example, a lane in Prestwick, in Ayrshire, is known locally as *The Puddock Sheuch* although this is not the name on the street-sign. It is no longer commonly frequented by puddocks (frogs/toads).

Strand – denoting the land bordering a river or the sea, this term is found in minor names and street-names of coastal areas, such as North and South Strand Street in Stranraer. The term is of uncertain origin, but is found in medieval Scottish texts dating back to the fifteenth century. Andrew of Wynton's *The Orygynale Cronykil of Scotland* (c.1420) describes how the River Nile bursts out

> *at the strande . . . by the Rede Se* [Red Sea].

Toll – as in English, a *toll* was a checkpoint on a turnpike road where monies were collected. This was also known as a *toll-bar*, a point not overlooked by punning publicans in more recent times. There are a large number of street-names and local names commemorating tolls. Examples include Eglinton Toll in Glasgow, Tollcross in Edinburgh, The Auld Toll on Stirling Road in Perthshire and The Toll at the boundary on the main road between Prestwick and Ayr in Ayrshire.

Tron – historically, this was the public steelyard or weighing-machine in a burgh, set up in or near the market-place for the weighing of various types of heavy or coarse goods. The district round about often became known as the Tron, and these areas have given rise to a variety of street-names such as Trongate in Glasgow. The Tron Kirk in Edinburgh was so named because of its proximity to the public weighing-machine. This public site was also the site of various forms of judicial punishment, some of which were particularly unpleasant. The records of Dundee Burgh Court note that, in 1550, an unfortunate by the name of Sandy Clerke was to be 'nalit [nailed] to the troyne be the ere [by the ear]'.

Umbrella – although this is not a particularly common term in place-names, there is a well-known bridge over Argyle Street in Glasgow that became known as the Hielanman's Umbrella in the early twentieth century. It supports part of Central Station and gained its name from its association with large numbers of Highland immigrants to Glasgow who were known to congregate under the bridge on wet evenings. Many of them worked in local shipyards. In 1999, the bridge received a Railway Heritage Award and a commemorative plaque plainly shows that this name is now official.

Vennel – this occurs in street-names throughout much of Scotland, including the Glasgow Vennel in Irvine, the Boat Vennel in Ayr, Friars Vennel in Dumfries, Northgate Vennel in Peebles and The Vennel in Edinburgh. The word derives from French *venelle* 'little street', and is found in Scots texts from the fifteenth century onwards. In the *Charters of the City of Edinburgh*, there are references to *the comon venale callit Sanct Leonardis wynde* and in the *Calendar of Writs preserved at Yester House* (1471), we find mention of *a venelle called Leichwynd.*

But caw canny — odd things can happen in vennels. The records of Perth Kirk Session for 1583–4 report that Walter Bog was *accused of cursing and biting of his mother-in-law . . . in the common vennell.*

Wynd – this term for a narrow, winding street or lane leading off a main road is often found in street-names such as Old Tolbooth Wynd in Edinburgh, Dyers Wynd in Paisley and Kirkland Wynd in Dumfries. The very oldest evidence for the Scots word comes from the names of streets recorded in Latin charter records from the thirteenth and fourteenth centuries. By the fifteenth century, far more documents were being written in Scots than Latin, and examples are more readily available. The *Charters of the City of Edinburgh* (1439) discuss

the comon venale callit Sanct Leonardis wynde

and the Burgh Records of Dunfermline (1488) give an account of payments of

annuel rent to Johne of Wallod of the Wynd.

If you are visiting any of Scotland's towns and cities,

look out for these words during your travels. You can encounter many of these terms, including closes, pends and vennels in the heart of Scotland's capital city, and if you stravaig further afield, there are many other visual signs of the living language. Although Scots terms are often anglicised when they occur in an official context — *raw* becoming *row* for instance — you may be surprised how much Scots is actually embedded in the names of everyday locations throughout the country.

Epilogue

I hope that you have enjoyed this exploration of the Scots language and the mark it has made on the landscape. Most of the quotations included in this book can also be found in the *Dictionary of the Scots Language*, which is what every good dictionary should be: an extraordinary storehouse of diverse and curious cultural information.

It's soon', no sense, that faddoms the herts o' men,
And by my sangs the rouch auld Scots I ken
E'en herts that ha'e nae Scots'll dirl richt thro'
As nocht else could — for here's a language rings
Wi datchie sesames, and names for nameless things.
(HUGH MCDIARMID, 'Gairmscoile', *Penny Wheep* (1926))